Passion for the Gospel

Hugh Latimer (1485–1555) Then and Now

A commemorative lecture to mark the 450th anniversary of his martyrdom in Oxford

Alister McGrath

Passion for the Gospel:
Hugh Latimer (1485-1555), Then and Now

A lecture given at St Andrew's Church, Oxford, on 12 October 2005 to mark the 450th anniversary of Latimer's martyrdom.

© 2005 by Alister E. McGrath
ISBN 0 946307 90 3

Published by the Latimer Trust
PO Box 26685
London N14 4XQ

www.latimertrust.org

Passion for the Gospel:
Hugh Latimer (1485-1555), Then and Now

Tonight we celebrate Hugh Latimer, sometime bishop of Worcester, remembered as one of three leading Protestant reformers martyred in this city of Oxford 450 years ago. Latimer was burned at the stake on 16 October 1555, along with his companion Nicholas Ridley, just outside Balliol College. A discrete cross in the street marks the spot. And, of course, a more substantial memorial, now renovated, now stands at the south end of St Giles. Shortly afterwards, Thomas Cranmer, the deposed archbishop of Canterbury, met the same fate. Latimer is remembered today chiefly for words he spoke to Ridley as the fires were lit beneath them: "Be of good comfort, Master Ridley, and play the man. We shall this day light up such a candle by God's grace in England as I trust shall never be put out!"

Tonight, we shall consider Latimer in more detail, for he deserves to be remembered for more than those words. If I may offer a modern parallel, we remember Dietrich Bonhoeffer – executed at Flossenburg in the closing months of the Second World War – for more than the remarkable calm and composure of his final days. Without in any way downplaying the importance of Bonhoeffer's witness to his faith through his death, we must remember that he was an able thinker, whose ideas can challenge and encourage us today. Indeed, his refusal to compromise on those ideas was the ultimate cause of his death.

Latimer, I believe, needs to be heard today, as do so many other voices from the sixteenth century. In this lecture, I hope to show ways in which Latimer can encourage us today, while at the same time unsettle us, by raising difficult questions that we sometimes prefer to ignore.

Let me begin by setting the context – that of the Reformation. This is a pivotal moment in the history of the western church, and has shaped much of the development of English Christianity ever since. The Reformation was fundamentally a quest for Christian identity and authenticity. It represents one of those great and rare moments in Christian history, when the church was prepared to re-examine itself. It was prepared to face up to a series of deeply disturbing questions concerning its role and its relevance. The Christian church has always been prone to a form of inertia, in the sense that there is a reluctance to adopt a *critical* attitude towards the ways things are, apparently on the basis of the assumption that what has happened is somehow *meant* to have happened. There is a reluctance to interrogate development, to challenge change.

And it is here that the Reformation had a fundamental contribution to make – a contribution which is continued in what has come to be known as "the Protestant principle". One of the deepest and most powerful wellheads which nourished the Reformation and its heritage is a spirit of creative protest, of prophetic criticism. This springs from the recognition of the sovereignty of God over his creation and his church, and of the living character of his revelation of himself in Jesus Christ and through scripture. This creative and critical principle is grounded in a dynamic understanding of God's self-revelation, and his call to the Christian church to re-examine and renew itself in its light. Classical evangelicalism has long been aware of the need for the community of faith continually to examine itself – its ideas, institutions, and actions – in the light of this revelation, leading to a characteristic pattern of scripture-nourished recovery, renewal and reform. That pattern first appears definitively at the time of the Reformation itself. There is much to be learned from the Reformation maxim *ecclesia reformata, ecclesia semper reformanda* – the reformed church must be a church which is always reforming itself. Reformation cannot be seen as a once for all event, now firmly located in the past. It must be a continuous process, not something that is over and done with.

The Reformation represented an overdue, and hence traumatic, questioning of unquestioned developments in Christian life and thought during the Middle Ages. It posed a challenge to the notion of the irreversibility of history, by suggesting that certain developments in the life and thought of the church during the Middle Ages were improper and illegitimate – and more than that: that they *could* and *should* be undone. The Reformation was a quest for Christian authenticity, based on the belief that the medieval church had lost its way and its reason for existence. It represented a willingness to take a profound risk – that of assuming that the foundational resources of the Christian faith could be recovered and applied to the strange world of the sixteenth century, and prove to be vital and relevant. Above all, the Reformation was a quest for Christian roots, grounded in the belief that a community which loses sight of its roots has lost sight of its reason for being in the world in the first place. And where do we find those roots? For the reformers, the answer was unequivocal: in the New Testament.

For Latimer and others, the Reformation was above all a quest of recovery and renewal – a recovery of the grounds of Christian identity, in the firm belief that recovery of identity led to renewal of purpose, and a recovery of vision. As we shall see, Latimer has much to say on this need for recovery of identity and vision, and the role of the Bible in creating and sustaining that vision.

But first, let us introduce Hugh Latimer, a son of the county of Leicestershire, born around the year 1485. Details of his early life are sketchy, and probably unreliable. Latimer was clearly academically able, and went up to Cambridge University. We know tantalisingly little of what he studied at Cambridge; we do know, however, that while still an undergraduate, he was elected a fellow of Clare College in 1510. By the early 1520s, Cambridge was known to be far more sympathetic to the ideas of the Reformation than Oxford. Luther's books, which had to be imported from continental Europe through the Flemish port of Antwerp, were much more accessible in Cambridge than Oxford. Many of the leading lights of the English Reformation had links with Cambridge around this time – most notably, Thomas Cranmer.

Much has been made of the circle of individuals who gathered at the "White Horse Tavern" at this time. This long-vanished public house is traditionally believed to have witnessed gatherings of those sympathetic to reform, much as the Inklings gathered at the "Eagle and Child" in St Giles. We know much less about this circle than we would like, and it is possible that it has been the subject of a little romantic embellishment here and there. Certainly, it features in John Foxe's famous *Book of Martyrs*. Yet however much historical truth may have been inflated at certain points, there is ample evidence that Martin Luther's books found their way to Cambridge, where they were read by many who were both attracted by his ideas, and interested in seeing whether they could be applied to the situation in England. Perhaps those conversations may have taken place in college rooms rather than public houses; nevertheless, they certainly took place.

Among those who began to ask questions about the possible reformation of the English church was Hugh Latimer. Latimer was initially hostile to the ideas of the Reformation.

In 1524, he defended a series of theses critical of the theology of Philip Melanchthon, Luther's second-in-command at Wittenberg. Indeed, Latimer seems to have criticised his Lutheran opponent with such success that some saw him as the man who might stem the tide of Lutheranism, then swelling in England, as it was elsewhere. Yet this Saul would in time become a Paul.

Traditionally – although the evidence is not as strong as we would like – Latimer was won over to the cause of the Reformation by Thomas Bilney, possibly in late 1524. We possess some sermons from the late 1520s which bear eloquent witness to his ability as a biblical preacher. Of these, the most interesting is the "Sermon on the Cards", preached in 1529, in which he likens the Christian life to a game of cards, dealt to us by God. His growing reputation attracted the attention of significant patrons within the English court, most notably Thomas Cromwell and Anne Boleyn, whose family had strong Protestant sympathies. In 1535, he was made Bishop of Worcester.

For several years, all seems to have been well. However, Henry VIII's religious policies were always somewhat unpredictable. At some points, he seemed sympathetic to Lutheranism – especially around the time of his divorce from Katherine of Aragon. At others, he seemed to lean in a more catholic direction. Latimer found himself caught up in one of these lurches. In 1539, believing that Henry's proposals for new articles of faith for the Church in England represented abandoning some fundamental Protestant principles, he resigned. He would never hold the office of bishop again, even though he was highly regarded throughout the reign of Edward VI.

We possess sermons from this period which give us a good indication of Latimer's reforming programme. Summarising it is no easy task, but one theme seems to me to dominate these sermons: to do and believe what the Bible teaches, and set to one side those things that are barriers to it. I have always felt that a phrase in John Foxe's famous account of Latimer's conversion to Protestantism in his *Book of Martyrs* is revealing. According to Foxe, Latimer "forsook the School doctors and other such fopperies and became an earnest student of true divinity". The word "foppery" means something that is excessively ornate. The implication is that an essentially simple gospel has been intellectually and culturally inflated, dressed up in extravagant, showy, worldly costume, where it ought to have been allowed to remain its simple self. This is one of the leading themes of Latimer's programme of reform – the elimination of ceremonies, practices and ideas which are not found in the Bible, or are not warranted by it. To some, it leads to a rather austere, forbidding form of Christianity – the sort that we associate with wearing black gowns. But for Latimer, both the church and the gospel had been distorted by additions, which eventually prevented the heart of the gospel from being discerned at all. What concerned Latimer was that human constructions – such as the elaborate ceremonies of the church, or the complex theological ideas of medieval scholasticism – were altogether obscuring the heart of the Christian faith. In his sermons of this period, we find Latimer demanding the ending and removal of such external trappings – such as elaborate clerical dress, or complex sacramental theatricalities. Simplicity was Latimer's watchword at this point.

So how was this return to the simple, unadorned, gospel to come about? Here we come to what is, in many ways, the lodestone of Latimer's thought – the centrality of the Bible, a leading theme of his sermons. To appreciate Latimer at this point, we need to remember something that is easily forgotten – the hostility towards translation of the Bible into English in the first part of Henry VIII's reign. Why was there such hostility? The answer is simple – power. Let's explore this further.

In 1520, Luther took the decisive steps which would lead to the fledgling Reformation breaking free from the limited confines of academia, and becoming a popular movement. He began writing works in German, rather than the more scholarly language of Latin, which was accessible only to an educated elite. Luther would continue to use Latin when it suited him; after all, he wanted his ideas to travel throughout Europe, and Latin was the cosmopolitan language of his day. Yet Latin was a language of exclusion, which ensured that common people could not share in the political and religious discussions of the élite. Luther chose the most accessible and inclusive language of the region to reinforce his message of reform. The arcane language of the church would be set aside, in order to allow Luther to speak directly to his fellow Germans in their native language.

Luther, however, recognised that language was not the only factor in reaching a wider audience. He needed to adapt his writing style as well. He therefore published three popular pamphlets in 1520, arguing the case for reform with wit and vigour. The first of these – *The Appeal to the German Nobility*, published in August 1520 – was perhaps the most important. In it, Luther set out – in German – the need for reform, and castigated the church and its clergy for their unwillingness to deal with the matter. So if the church would not reform itself, what could be done? Luther's answer was as simple as it was radical: the German laity should press for the reform that the church sought to evade.

Luther now added a more fundamental demand. The laity should have the right to read and interpret the Bible for themselves. Why should they depend on the Pope to interpret the Bible for them? Were there not vested interests here? What was special about the Pope, anyway?

And why did the Bible have to be locked away from the people, imprisoned in the fetters of a dead language which only a charmed circle could read? Why could not the educated laity be allowed to read the Bible in their own languages for themselves, and form judgements on whether what the church taught and practiced was in line with the biblical material?

Erasmus had produced a new Latin translation of the New Testament. That was useful. But most laity could not read this learned language – what *they* needed was the New Testament to be translated accurately into the language they used in their everyday lives. Giving the laity access to the Bible in their own language would let them see how they had been duped by the clergy. Having realised the need for such a translation, Luther decided the task was too important to leave to anyone else. He would do it himself, and translated the New Testament into German.

Making the Bible available in the German language thus became a priority. Luther argued that the medieval church had built walls around the Bible, in an attempt to exclude ordinary Christians from reading and interpreting it. The Bible was treated as a fortified city, with walls designed to keep the ordinary people out. Luther saw himself as a latter-day Joshua. He would cause the walls of this new Jericho to come tumbling down. The medieval church, he argued, tried to exclude the laity from reading the Bible, by preventing it from being read in a language they could understand. He, Luther, would change all that. The Bible would be available in German! And so the massive task began, in which Luther would painstakingly translate the Bible from its original languages into the everyday language of his people.

By 1525, Luther was widely seen as the leading light of the growing movement for reform within the western European church. His ideas were being debated and discussed across

Europe. Two ideas can be seen as underlying both his critique of the church and his proposals for reform. First, the church had lost sight of the basic New Testament idea that salvation is given by God as a gift, not earned as a reward. Second, the key to the reform and renewal of the church was to put the Bible in the hands of lay people. This second idea was set out with especial force in his 1520 writing *The Appeal to the German Nobility*. The key to the reform of the church and the correction of its errors lay in increasing biblical literacy.

If the Bible was available in the vernacular, everyone could read it and judge the teachings of the church for themselves. Power could thus pass from the hierarchy of the church to its ordinary people. The Reformation could thus be seen as a movement of popular empowerment, in which the laity would be given the right to judge the church, and demand its reform and renewal. Not surprisingly, this was seen as profoundly threatening by the church establishment, which promptly made every attempt it could to suppress Luther's ideas.

Latimer, as we would expect, was a powerful supporter of the cause of biblical translation. The Bible needed to be made available and accessible to every Christian man and woman, whatever their social status. This was about the democratisation of faith, the enabling of ordinary Christians to read the Bible without someone looking over their shoulders, telling them what to believe and how to interpret. It is a powerful theme, which many today still find unsettling. Many clergy would much prefer that their congregations merely listened to their interpretations of the Bible. Luther and Latimer would have every Christian read the Bible for themselves, and challenge their clergy on their interpretation as appropriate. It is highly doubtful whether the reformers envisaged the emergence of a new professional class of biblical interpreters, who relieved their people of the need to think for themselves!

Latimer is thought to have been the author of one of the most important of the Homilies – a collection of authorised sermons, which clergy were required to preach from time to time under the reign of Edward VI. The evidence for this authorship is insecure; however, the ideas we find in that homily are unquestionably Latimer's. I propose to explore these ideas with you tonight.

Let us begin by asking why these homilies played such an important role in consolidating the Protestant heritage of the Church of England, initially during the reign of Edward VI, and later during the reign of Elizabeth I. Latimer begins this opening homily of this collection by setting out the central role of Scripture in the Christian life:

> To a Christian man there can be nothing either more necessary or profitable, than the knowledge of holy Scripture, forasmuch as in it is contained God's true word, setting forth his glory, and also man's duty. . . . Therefore as many as be desirous to enter into the right and perfect way unto God, must apply their minds to know holy Scripture, without the which, they can neither sufficiently know God and his will, neither their office and duty.

We see immediately two themes – the evocation of the glory of God, and the establishment of our responsibilities, not merely towards God, but to our neighbours and society as a whole. Latimer shares in the conviction of his age, that every aspect of the world is to be ordered according to God's will, and that this will can be discerned from a prayerful and obedient reading of Scripture. Warming to his theme, he continues as follows:

> For in holy Scripture is fully contained what we ought to do, and what to eschew; what to believe, what to love, and what to look for at God's hands at length. In these Books we shall find the father from whom, the son by whom, and the holy Ghost, in whom all

things have their being and keeping up, and these three persons to be but one GOD, and one substance. In these books we may learn to know our selves, how vile and miserable we be, and also to know God, how good he is of himself, and how he maketh us and all creatures partakers of his goodness.

We see here an insight characteristic of the Christian faith — that it is in knowing God and knowing ourselves that true wisdom is to be found. The form of spirituality that is characteristic of the Protestant Reformation insists that the quest for human identity, authenticity and fulfilment cannot be undertaken in isolation from God. To find out *who* we are — and *why* we are — is to find out who God is, and what he is like. John Calvin states this principle with characteristic lucidity some years later in the opening sentence of the 1559 edition of his *Institutes of the Christian Religion*:

> Nearly all the wisdom we possess, that is to say, true and sound wisdom, consists of two parts: the knowledge of God and of ourselves. And although they are closely connected, it is difficult to say which comes first... Knowledge of ourselves not only stimulates us to seek God but, as it were, also leads us by the hand to find him. . . . We never achieve a clear knowledge of ourselves until we have first looked upon God's face, and then descend from contemplating him to examine ourselves.

Any notion of the Christian life as a quest for heightened religious experience as an end in itself is totally alien to the outlook of the Reformation. Equally, any idea that it is possible to have a detached or disinterested knowledge of God is excluded. To know God is to be changed by God. Latimer anticipates Calvin's fuller statement of this point in his homily, and we should listen to him carefully. Today's culture presents us with a myriad of understandings of how to achieve authentic existence, or to become the person we really are, and so on. Underlying all of these is that most fundamental question: what is the ultimate ground and the ultimate goal of human nature? Latimer suggests that we discover the biblical notion that our true being, identity and destiny lie in our relationship with God as creator and redeemer – and having discovered this, that we should trust it, and act upon its basis.

Latimer invites us to discover the sheer pleasure of reading Scripture, using biblical imagery intended to whet our appetites:

> These Books therefore ought to bee much in our hands, in our eyes, in our ears, in our mouths, but most of all in our hearts. For the Scripture of God is the heavenly meat of our souls (Matthew 4.4), the hearing and keeping of it maketh us blessed (Luke 11.28), sanctifieth us (John 17.17), and maketh us holy, it turneth our souls (Psalms 19.7-10), it is a light lantern to our feet (Psalms 119.105), it is a sure, stedfast, and everlasting instrument of salvation, it giveth wisdom to the humble and lowly hearts, it comforteth, maketh glad, cheereth, and cherisheth our conscience: it is a more excellent jewel or treasure, then any gold or precious stone, it is more sweet then honey, or honey-combe, it is called the best part, which Mary did choose, for it hath in it everlasting comfort (Luke 10.42).

But while the Bible offers us much comfort, it also challenges us. Latimer was one of the most vociferous critics of the church in his lifetime, and some of the criticisms that he makes were uncomfortable for those who heard them in his day, and remain so today. Those of us who are Protestants will feel quite at ease with his critique of extravagant clergy dress, of ritualised worship, of heavily orchestrated performances of the Lord's Supper, and of the power and authority of the Pope. But what of other criticisms he directs against those prominent in church and society? In 1548, during Edward's brief reign, Latimer preached at St Paul's Cross, in London. His sermon was a searing indictment of the social inequality of England. With the power of a prophet – the sermon draws on Old Testament roots – Latimer lambasted those who sought to become rich, or stay rich, while failing to care for the poor or do anything to better their plight. These words are typical:

> You landlords, you rent-raisers, you have for your possession too much. . . . and thus is caused such dearth, that poor men that live on their labour cannot with the sweat of their faces have their living. . . . The enhancing and bearing goes all to your private commodity and wealth. Ye had a single too much, and now ye have a double too much; but let the preacher preach till his tongue be worn to a stump, nothing is amended. This one thing I tell you, from whom it cometh, I know, even from the Devil.

Especially in the United States, but also here in England, many of today's largest evangelical churches are reluctant to preach on the biblical condemnation of excessive wealth, in that they need their congregation's financial support for their evangelistic or didactic programmes. It is not the happiest of situations. Can our churches exercise a genuinely prophetic voice in such situations, when so much that goes on within our churches depends upon maintaining the goodwill of wealthy congregation members? I have no answer, I fear, but I know that Latimer would wish us to ask that question.

Latimer, as we have seen, emphasised the centrality of the Bible to the Christian life. This was a common theme of Protestantism at this time, as can be seen from the literary resources made available by the major reformers for their followers. Three are of especial importance.

1. The *biblical commentary* aimed to allow its readers to peruse and understand the word of God, explaining difficult phrases, identifying points of importance, and generally allowing its readers to become familiar with the thrust and concerns of the biblical passage. Writers such as John Calvin and Martin Luther produced commentaries aimed at a variety of readerships, both academic and lay.

2. The *expository sermon* aimed to fuse the horizons of the scriptural texts and its hearers, applying the principles underlying the scriptural passage to the situation of the audience. Calvin's sermons at Geneva are a model of continuous preaching through a scriptural book, rather than on passages drawn from a lectionary or chosen by the preacher. For example, during the period between 20 March 1555 to 15 July 1556, Calvin is known to have preached some two hundred sermons on a single scriptural book – Deuteronomy.

3. Works of *biblical theology*, especially Calvin's *Institutes of the Christian Religion*, aimed to allow their readers to gain an appreciation of the theological coherence of scripture, by bringing together and synthesising its statements on matters of theological importance. By doing this, it enabled its readers to establish a coherent and consistent world-view, which would undergird their everyday lives.

It has often been a matter of comment that the English Reformation did not produce anything like as many works of this kind as we might expect, if we use the continental reformers as a yardstick. Certainly, Latimer and his colleagues showed themselves to be able theologians, and had no difficulty in developing what we recognise as biblical approaches to both theology and to the tasks of Christian living. Yet it is not done as systematically, as intentionally, as we find elsewhere. Why not?

The answer is perhaps to be found in the rather different situations confronted by reformers in Germany and England. As has often been pointed out, theology mattered to the German Reformation. From its outset, that Reformation was about reforming a church through theological reflection, creating a new sense of identity and purpose. The English Reformation was more pragmatic; theology did not matter so much. The English church was already defined culturally, so there was little need to repeat Luther's theological system-building in Germany, or Calvin's in Geneva. Indeed, so underdeveloped was English Protestant theology during the 1540s that Thomas Cranmer called in leading lights of the continental Reformation – Peter Martyr Vermigli in Oxford, and Martin Bucer in Cambridge – to try to sort things out. The judgement of history is that the revival of theology in England belongs to a later generation. It is the seventeenth, rather than the sixteenth, century, which produced the most significant Anglican and Puritan theology. Latimer, we must remember, is to be seen in his historical context, and is not to be criticised for doing something that was not seen to be of decisive importance in his day. Latimer was one who loved, preached and applied the Bible, but did not see the construction of theological systems as part of his task – or anyone else's at that time.

So how might we relate Latimer to our own day and age – a time of confusion, bewilderment, uncertainty and hostility, paralleling in so many ways those difficult and dangerous days of the early English Reformation. I have already spoken of Latimer encouraging and rebuking us, and stressing the importance of the Bible. But how might he help us address our own situation? In this lecture, I have time to address one, and only one, topic. I have therefore chosen something that I believe to be important, just as I know it is difficult. The topic is the limits of divergence and tolerance within the church.

This has been a subject of debate since the Donatist controversy of the patristic era, and it simply will not go away because it is such a deep, difficult and divisive issue, where there seem to be no absolute boundary markers. We can be tolerant, and suggest that, as long as we all love the Lord, we don't need to worry too much about anything else. The early church soon found out that there was a lot else to worry about, as inadequate or downright mistaken understandings of the identity of Jesus Christ began to threaten the church's future. Unless we understand Jesus as he truly is, the church cannot hope to survive, let alone to prosper. We must draw lines somewhere – not because we want to be awkward or difficult, but because we need to safeguard the treasure that has been passed down to us. The church cannot survive on a faulty vision of its own foundation and calling. We must safeguard what has been entrusted to us – a theme which is of major importance in the later writings of the New Testament, especially the epistles to Timothy and Titus.

Yet we all know what happens if you draw lines or defend them too vigorously. You encourage the emergence of a heresy-hunting mindset, where any deviation from what your particular circle regards as orthodoxy leads to expulsion and isolation. You end up looking for even the most minute disagreement or error, instead of celebrating the gospel that binds us together. The dangers of this have frequently been emphasised by J. I. Packer, who has written of a trend which he saw as being "near to being a cultic heresy"– a doctrine of "justification, not by works, but by words – words, that is, of notional soundness and precision". Packer pointed out how "it is the way of fundamentalists to follow the path of contentious orthodoxism, as if the mercy of God in Christ automatically rests on persons who are notionally correct and is just as automatically withheld from those who fall short of notional correctness on any point of substance." It is a view just as inadequate and objectionable as the first – but where are we to draw the line? Is there a middle way? Can there be a generous orthodoxy, prepared to take its stands on essentials, yet to be generous and tolerant on inessentials?

Latimer knew this problem well. We see it emerging during his time as Bishop of Worcester under Henry VIII, when it is clear that he had to behave in ways that were not entirely to his liking. Henry may have been sympathetic to at least some themes of the Reformation agenda; he was certainly not going to change the liturgical practices or structures of the church. He may have substituted his own authority for that of the Pope; he was not, however, prepared to buy into Lutheran theology to any significant extent. Latimer's appointment as Bishop of Worcester caused him some difficulties, in that he was under an obligation to undertake certain ceremonies which, for a Protestant, might seem pointless or simply wrong. John Foxe, however, places a particular spin on this period in his *Book of Martyrs*, which encourages us to see his compliance in a generally benevolent light:

> Guided by Providence, he escaped the subtle nets of his persecutors, and at length, through the powerful friends before mentioned, became bishop of Worcester, in which function he qualified or explained away most of the papal ceremonies he was for form's sake under the necessity of complying with.

What we see here is not a cheap unprincipled compromise, but a judicious decision which was, in many ways, typical of the age. The opportunity to advance the cause of Protestantism in the long term through such high office was seen as outweighing the difficulties caused by being obliged to accept certain theological, ecclesiastical and liturgical positions which were not of his own choosing.

But there were limits, and those limits were reached for Latimer with the publication of the Six Articles in 1539. The English Reformation seemed to have gone into reverse gear, moving away from the Protestant principles that seemed to have been introduced some years earlier. No longer could Latimer defend his position of working within the system. He resigned. The pressure increased under Mary Tudor, when he was called upon to recant his Protestantism. Once more, Latimer knew that there were limits, and declined to do so, knowing what the consequences would be. The principle was clear: one may graciously give way on certain points, in return for advancing a reforming agenda. But Latimer was not prepared to compromise beyond his limits, either in relation to his job, or his life. The debate continues today over what those limits should be. There are many who share Latimer's dilemma, and will also share his pain and despair over what is to be done. Latimer may not give us answers on this one, but he certainly gives us a role model as we wrestle with such difficult questions.

I have already hinted at Latimer's end, and we must now turn to finish our story. Although Latimer had played a relatively small role in the consolidation of the Protestant Reformation under Edward VI, his influence and prominence was sufficient to draw attention to him under the reign of Mary Tudor. Had Edward VI lived to be an old man, the course of English history might have been rather different. As it was, the process of consolidating Protestantism was still at an early stage when Edward died. Under the terms of Henry VIII's will, his successor was Mary Tudor, his daughter by Katherine of Aragon. While there is some uncertainty over what Mary Tudor intended to do through her religious policies, one of the most persuasive means of interpreting them is to see them as trying to reconstitute the Catholic church in England, not so much as it had been under her father Henry VIII, but as it had been *before* him.

Some Protestants who posed an obstacle to this retrogression were eliminated through imprisonment. Those who could afford to often chose to flee to the great Protestant cities of Europe. The so-called "Marian exiles" found refuge in Geneva, Zurich, Frankfurt and Strasbourg. On their return to England after Mary's death, they brought first-hand knowledge of working Protestant communities to their homeland, ensuring that Elizabethan England would be shaped by their vision of the Reformation. But that lay in the future. Others found that their refusal to give way on what they regarded as Protestant non-negotiables led to their execution. Among them was Latimer, who is rightly remembered as one of the most significant martyrs of the English Reformation. Historians generally regard Mary's decision to persecute leading Protestants as a serious error of judgement. The execution of Thomas Cranmer in particular was viewed with revulsion by many, and helped create the impression that Catholicism was being imposed by force, with the assistance of Spanish influence.

But I must end. I have spoken of Latimer as a representative of the Reformation, inviting us to constantly examine our thoughts and actions in the light of Scripture, and being prepared to change, reform and renew where necessary. To return to the Reformation is to recapture that sense of evangelical simplicity, creativity, freshness and vivacity which later generations often seem unwittingly to have forfeited, sometimes without realising it. The Reformation possesses a remarkable ability to surprise and delight those who have been brought up within the framework of later forms of Protestantism, gently challenging them to reconsider and reinvigorate their thinking.

Latimer, I think, says much to encourage us – but also much that will unsettle us. I hope we will listen to him, and not dismiss him as a voice from a long-dead past. He has much to say to us about how to live and die. I hope and pray that we who live in less oppressive times than Latimer, Ridley or Cranmer may still feel that we have something that is worth living and dying for. For what good is life, if we have not yet found something that is worth dying for? And what better thing to die for, than the gospel of the one who first died for us?

Suggestions for Further Reading

Latimer's sermons can be found in many editions, including:

Latimer, Hugh. *Selected Sermons of Hugh Latimer.* Charlottesville, VA: University of Virginia Press, 1968.

Latimer, Hugh. *Sermons by Hugh Latimer.* Lewes, West Sussex: Focus Christian Ministries Trust, 1987.

For secondary studies, see:

Chester, Allan Griffith. *Hugh Latimer : Apostle to the English.* Philadelphia: University of Pennsylvania Press, 1954.

Dickens, A. G. *The English Reformation.* 2nd ed. London: Batsford, 1989.

Gray, Charles M. *Hugh Latimer and the Sixteenth Century : An Essay in Interpretation.* Cambridge, MA: Harvard University Press, 1950.

Loades, David M. *The Oxford Martyrs.* London: Batsford, 1970.

MacCulloch, Diarmaid. *Thomas Cranmer : A Life.* New Haven, CT: Yale University Press, 1996.

For J.I. Packer's reflections on the problem of "justification by words", see his essay "On from Orr: The Cultural Crisis, Rational Realism, and Incarnational Ontology." *Crux* 32, no. 3 (1996): 12-26.